Places in my community

Bobbie Kalman

🍄 Crabtree Publishing Company

www.crabtreebooks.com

Created by Bobbie Kalman

Author and Editor-in-Chief
Bobbie Kalman

Educational consultants
Reagan Miller
Joan King
Elaine Hurst

Editors
Reagan Miller
Joan King
Kathy Middleton

Proofreader
Crystal Sikkens

Design
Bobbie Kalman
Katherine Berti

Photo research
Bobbie Kalman

Production coordinator
Katherine Berti

Prepress technician
Katherine Berti

Photographs
All photographs by Shutterstock except:
Comstock: p. 13 (bottom left)

Library and Archives Canada Cataloguing in Publication

Kalman, Bobbie, 1947-
    Places in my community / Bobbie Kalman.

(My world)
Includes index.
ISBN 978-0-7787-9443-1 (bound).--ISBN 978-0-7787-9487-5 (pbk.)

    . Community life--Juvenile literature.
I. Title. II. Series: My world (St. Catharines, Ont.)

HM761.K34 2010   j307   C2009-906103-1

Library of Congress Cataloging-in-Publication Data

Kalman, Bobbie.
 Places in my community / Bobbie Kalman.
    p. cm. -- (My world)
 Includes index.
  ISBN 978-0-7787-9487-5 (pbk. : alk. paper) -- ISBN 978-0-7787-9443-1
 (reinforced library binding : alk. paper)
 1. Community life--Juvenile literature. I. Title. II. Series.

 HM761.K35 2010
 307--dc22
                                                         2009041222

Crabtree Publishing Company

Printed in the U.S.A./112013/CG20130917

www.crabtreebooks.com   1-800-387-7650

Published in Canada
Crabtree Publishing
616 Welland Ave.
St. Catharines, Ontario
L2M 5V6

Published in the United States
Crabtree Publishing
PMB 59051
350 Fifth Avenue, 59th Floor
New York, New York 10118

Published in the United Kingdom
Crabtree Publishing
Maritime House
Basin Road North, Hove
BN41 1WR

Published in Australia
Crabtree Publishing
3 Charles Street
Coburg North
VIC, 3058

What is in this book?

What is a community?

A **community** is a place where many people live and work together.
A community has many buildings.
It also has outdoor places like parks.
What are some places in your community?

A community **neighborhood** is where people live.
Communities also have playgrounds, schools,
stores, and fire stations.

Places to live

Homes are buildings.

There are many kinds of homes.

Some homes have one or two floors.

Other homes are in tall **apartment** buildings.
Each building has many apartment homes.

Places to work

People in a community work to earn money.
They earn money to pay for food,
clothing, and other things they need.
People do many kinds of jobs.
Some people work outdoors.

Some people work in **factories**.
These workers are making cars.

Places to learn

Communities have schools for learning. Young children go to **elementary school**. Older students go to **high school** or **college**. Which kind of school do you go to?

School is a place to learn and have fun.
You can do art and music at school.
You can play sports, too.

Places to buy food

People need food to stay alive.

Most people buy food at a **supermarket**.

You can buy any kind of food there.

You can also buy food
in restaurants.

Many people grow
vegetable gardens.
Do you have a
vegetable garden?

Places to shop

People need other things, such as clothes, books, toys, and computers. You can find many of these things in **shopping malls**.

Shopping malls have
different kinds of stores.
This girl bought a lot
of things at the mall.

Community safety

Communities need to be safe.
Police officers help keep communities safe.
People call the **police station** when they need help.

police station

Firefighters put out fires.
They wait at a **fire station**
until someone reports a fire.
Then they drive to the fire in
fire trucks that have loud **sirens**.

Places to get well

Communities help people stay healthy. People go to a doctor's office when they are sick or to get checkups. They go to a **hospital** when they are hurt or very sick.

There are animal hospitals, too.
Doctors called **veterinarians**,
or vets, look after animals
that are sick or hurt.

Long ago

Do you like to draw and paint?
Art galleries show pictures
that people have painted.
Some of the paintings show
how children lived long ago.

Museums show how people and animals live now and long ago. This museum has dinosaur bones. Dinosaurs lived a very long time ago!

Fun places outdoors

Communities have many fun places. There are parks, playgrounds, sports fields, and swimming pools. Where do you have fun in your community?

Words to know and Index

food
pages 12–13

homes
pages 6–7

hospitals
pages 18–19

museums
pages 20–21

outdoor fun
pages 4, 5, 22–23

safety
pages 5, 16–17

schools
pages 5, 10–11

shopping malls
pages 5, 14–15

work places
pages 8–9